"Practical and spiritual, heart-warming and affectionate, these r[illegible]tions on the cross will be enjoyed over a good cup of coffee, i[illegible] of your home, when traveling, or anywhere and by an[illegible]o find gospel solace in our sometimes confuse[illegible]

JOSH MOODY, Se[illegible]

"Wil and Lorraine Triggs's *The Wondro*[illegible]pel-spring in your step throughout the day, as it leads yo[illegible]rkan trail from the transfiguration to the cross. The authors' bri[illegible]d penetrating reflections contain some surprising turns that will both delight and convict. This is, at once, a winsome and serious book—full of good cheer, perfect for Lent and any other season."

R. KENT HUGHES, Former Professor of Practical Theology at Westminster Theological Seminary; Senior Pastor Emeritus, College Church, Wheaton

"*The Wondrous Cross* is a proverbial breath of fresh air. It rises above the conventional book of devotionals with its variety, creativity, and real-life authenticity. It is both edifying and what is familiarly called a page-turner (a book that invites you to keep reading). It offers two for the price of one—forty days of daily Lenten devotionals, and a book that you can read with edification and delight in one or two sittings any time of the year."

LELAND RYKEN, Professor Emeritus, Wheaton College and Author

THE

WONDROUS

CROSS

THE WONDROUS CROSS

REAL LIFE REFLECTIONS FROM THE TRANSFIGURATION TO THE CROSS

WIL & LORRAINE TRIGGS

10 Publishing
a division of 10 of those.com

First published in Great Britain in 2026

British Library Cataloguing in Publication Data
A record for this book is available from the British Library

EU GPSR: 6b Upper Water Street, Newry, Northern Ireland, BT34 1DJ

ISBN: 978-1-83728-163-3

Designed by Jude May
Cover image © Anastasiia Zvonary | iStock
Printed in Denmark

10Publishing, a division of 10ofthose.com
Unit C, Tomlinson Road, Leyland, PR25 2DY

info@10ofthose.com
www.10ofthose.com

1 3 5 7 10 8 6 4 2

This book is dedicated to all the children we've taught, and their parents and grandparents. Thank you for sharing life with us.

Introduction

There are a few things you should know before you read this book.

Confession: neither of us comes from faith traditions that observe Lent. Forty readings for the days leading up to Easter sounds like a Lenten devotional and this book can be used between Ash Wednesday and Easter Sunday. Since Sundays are excluded from the forty days of Lent, each Sunday you may like to spend some time praying and reflecting on the previous week of devotions. You could also use this resource in the days following Easter or any season of the year. There is no time of year when reading Scripture, praying to God and living the gospel are out of season. These actions are always good, and we should do them often in all seasons.

The gospel changes everything. At least, it should. The gospel, the good news, is *why* Jesus died on the cross and then rose back to life. But Jesus and his Spirit also shape *how* the gospel transforms us and the world around us. This shaping happens in quiet and often unexpected ways. Our prayer is that this journey will infuse the gospel with new life in you, and through you to the world around you. Dare to let God bring light to your heart, your day, your people, your world.

In these forty readings we walk through the life of Jesus from his transfiguration to the cross. We will use the Gospel of Mark's narrative as our anchor, with side trails to the other Gospels and the Old Testament.

After all, all of Scripture points to Jesus. These devotional readings are meant to help in deepening our commitment to Jesus Christ through giving greater attention to God, to his created world and to the people around us.

At the end of each chapter, we give an action point in one of these three areas:

1. **Pray out loud:** Say a prayer to Jesus. Say it out loud when no one but he can hear. You can pray the words in our devotionals or use them as a springboard to talk to Jesus from your heart. Vocalizing prayer uses our body more fully than an internal prayer of unspoken thoughts.

2. **Crossroad:** Repentance means stop, turn around, follow Jesus. How might God be calling you to turn around and change course, to confess sin and find his forgiveness, and to walk more fully in his path?

3. **All things new:** Take a generous look outward. See afresh the people and the world around you. Embrace these in new ways as we together approach the cross of Jesus.

The Wondrous Cross, our title, comes from one of our favorite songs of this season, "When I Survey the Wondrous Cross." Written in 1707 by Isaac Watts, this hymn is one we sing every year. Originally a symbol of shame and humiliation, the cross Jesus bore for us became a place of wonder and surprise. The surprise, the joy, is that Jesus brings eternal life and truth in unexpected ways—humility over pride; sacrifice over subjugation; a mule instead of a stallion. It's always unexpected, yet it is thrillingly right and true. This comes to life in our lives in individual Spirit-guided ways.

Let's walk this path together, drawing nearer to the cross and finding a wonder that is beautifully not our own.

1

My Favorite Stuffies

Typically, at the start of the school year, stuffies (stuffed animals) show up to our Sunday school for five- and six-year-olds. We never turn away stuffies of any color, critter or costume.

I understand this attachment to stuffies. When my son was young, his treasured Winnie-the-Pooh stuffie came with him on a family weekend in Chicago. We had checked out of the hotel when our son wailed, "I left Pooh Bear in the room."

In seconds, the concierge and the front desk became involved in our family drama to retrieve Winnie-the-Pooh. When the concierge announced that Pooh Bear had been reunited with his family, everyone applauded.

I thought of stuffies when I read 2 Chronicles 13 for my Bible study. Abijah, king of Judah, and Jeroboam, king of Israel, were at war when Abijah questioned Jeroboam's battle plan: "And now you think to withstand the kingdom of the LORD in the hand of the sons of David, because you are a great multitude and have with you the golden calves that Jeroboam made you for gods" (v. 8).

It probably comes from hanging out with young children, but I started to laugh as I imagined Jeroboam's warriors with their little golden-calf stuffies tucked under their arms—too attached to leave them behind.

I wish I could laugh at the stuffies in my life, but like those mighty warriors, I am too attached to them to leave them behind. One favorite stuffie is Creature Comfort. Then there's the twin stuffies Achievement and Accolade. The coolest stuffie talks, and her name is Miss Opinion. When paired with Bluetooth, she can come with me anywhere, anytime. Oh, how I love Miss Opinion.

Your stuffie collection might be different from mine, but not our shared attachment to them. It's the attachment that tethers us to the here and now, to what we can see and to what we think we control. Our gaze is distinctly horizontal, looking for a human savior to rescue us.

In his book, *The Heart in Pilgrimage*, Leland Ryken features a devotional by Richard Baxter, "The Saints' Everlasting Rest." Stuffies probably weren't on Baxter's mind when he wrote this devotional, but he did offer a solution for our attachment to them: look up to our eternal rest. Baxter wrote, "take one walk every day in the new Jerusalem." He calls to mind Daniel, who "in his captivity, daily opened his window toward Jerusalem, though far out of sight, he went to God in his devotions; so may the believing soul, in this captivity of the flesh, look toward Jerusalem which is above."[1]

Crossroad

Perhaps the best way to prepare for resurrection—both Christ's and our promised one—is to escape from our captivity by opening our windows and taking a daily walk in Jerusalem. What windows do you need to open to take that walk today?

For further reading: Daniel 6:10, 23-27.

2

I Give Up

A good friend's Facebook post upset me. It wasn't about me, but about something close to my heart. That hurt. So, I decided to tell him, ironically, by text.

He explained that this post was his way of finding truth, but he was sorry; I mattered to him more than any truth he was looking for on social media posts. He also said he was going to give up social media for Lent.

Ah, giving up things. In ancient times, people sacrificed to appease gods, even and especially the false ones. When people talk of their denials today, it seems more like the path to a pagan temple than a life-changing road to Calvary.

Yet Lent give-ups are temporary; they only last until Easter Sunday. Nor can we fallen humans sacrifice like God did. It's impossible. We can't atone or intercede. And the finished work of Jesus means we don't have to.

That's why I'm giving up on giving up.

Instead I'll take hold of something new. Maybe I'm going to take hold of prayer, speaking to God audibly when no one else is around to hear. Or perhaps in church on Sunday, I'm going to make eye contact and listen. Someone is waiting to hear hello, pray together, be the messenger. Help me find that person and not look away.

Life is the anti-Groundhog Day. Every day is new. There are no repeats.

As I give up giving up, my heart-battered, head-throbbing soul cries out: Be on the lookout for Jesus today; let the Word explain himself along the way—what he does, who he is. It is to be like a ewe lamb that is lost, then found; to drink cool water from the still waters; to eat like one who has not eaten in forever; it is to lap up, like water or bloody meat, from the lowest manger.

I will not give up on him who has taken all my sin completely to the utmost—drinking the cup only he could hold. The Potter could mold the chalice; swallow the dregs to the very last breath; and then fold the linen graveclothes when he was done with death.

I long to see Jesus. I long to be like the disciples who recognize him again, hear the not-me word when he breaks the bread and remember how he appears in their midst like he had never gone—because he never had and never will. Still Jesus is here—in word and flesh; he will always be ever nearer than near.

Pray out loud

Jesus' love is wondrous to behold, yet beyond us—even us in his grasp. Down he reaches, beyond the farthest, to find farther fathoms further down; down he bends. He travels on foot beyond the very last bend.

Take my hand, my dear ones; we've a wedding to attend.

For further reading: Psalm 40:3-8; Ephesians 2:8-9.

3

Off My Pedestal

Forget Queen Victoria and even William Shakespeare. On this London trip, as a Sunday school curriculum editor at the time, I wanted to find one statue—Robert Raikes, the founder of the modern-day Sunday school movement.

My husband spotted the statue first—in the shade of the Victoria Embankment Gardens, behind The Savoy. The description on the base read: "Robert Raikes/Founder of Sunday Schools/1780. This statue was erected under the direction of the Sunday School Union by contributions from teachers and scholars of the Sunday Schools in Great Britain."

I imagined Sunday school teachers encouraging the children to bring in coins to help build the statue, then organizing a field trip to see it.

Whether you like statues or not, we do like having control of who we place on our pedestals—flawed people elevating other flawed people to almost God-like statuses. We like to elevate ourselves and others.

In Mark 9:2-8, Jesus' transfiguration has an ordinary beginning: "... Jesus took with him Peter and James and John, and led them up a high mountain." Then the most extraordinary event took place: they saw Jesus' glory. They saw Moses and Elijah talking with Jesus. They saw glory, and said ... let's build tents, three tents.

I think Mark was being generous when he noted that Peter "did not know what to say" (Mark 9:6). God had the final say in the cloud on top of the mountain: "This is my beloved Son, listen to him!" (v. 7). Jesus is greater than Elijah, greater than Moses. He cannot be contained in any tent or statue. But a few verses later, the disciples were ready to unpack the other two tents as they argued about which of them was the greatest—which of them deserved the statue, or should I say status. I would have been right in the thick of that argument.

About eight days before the transfiguration, Jesus said, "If anyone would come after me, let him deny himself and take up his cross and follow me" (Mark 8:34). Jesus didn't say *climb up on a pedestal*, but *take up your cross*. Lose your life to save it.

There's one other thing Jesus wants us to take up—his kind yoke and light burden—as we learn from his gentle and lowly heart. He wants to remove our burdens and give us rest for our souls.

I must rest from pitching that tent for my current idol, rest from that next time I kick the base of my pedestal—tempted to climb back up—and rest from trying to earn his grace or prove myself to him.

Jesus sees and loves us. His unwavering presence is the path to hope and change. The cross, the empty tomb and the words in Scripture are enough—not etched in a monument, but written on our hearts by the nail-scarred hands of God himself.

All things new

What pedestal do you need to climb down from?

For further reading: Mark 8:34–37.

4

The Twins

My dad was a twin. I never met that uncle; he died before I came along. Yet Aunt Alberta was a storyteller, and she enraptured me with stories of growing up in Nebraska cornfields. When she came to town for Dad's funeral, she told us the way Dad saved her from harm. She stepped into a metal milking can and couldn't get out. She was terrified. My dad figured out a way to free her. He saved her, she said.

She also recalled that it was a big deal in their little town when twins were born. Back then people thought that there was a good twin and a bad twin. We know that this is not true. Everyone is born in sin, but also capable of good. Did my dad believe that he was the bad twin? The good one? Which would be worse? Did he carry that question with him throughout his life? Did such thinking adversely affect their sibling relationship or the way they thought about themselves?

There is another kind of good/bad twin syndrome that we each carry all the time. We face twin responses: one is good; the other not so much.

Turning the other cheek or smacking the other guy in the face. Respecting your boss or giving him a piece of your mind. Belief or unbelief. It isn't doubleminded to struggle in this way, but there's always a choice.

Mark 9:14-29 tells of a father who believed enough to bring his son to

Jesus. He had previously watched the disciples heal other people, but when they came to this man and his son, nothing happened.

Then there was a dispute among the crowd. There are no details, but I imagine people were telling the father to give up and go home—to make room for others. Give up.

He didn't leave. There was enough belief to stay. Jesus came and they talked the situation over.

"If you can do anything, have compassion on us and help us," the father said.

Jesus responded, "If you can! All things are possible for the one who believes."

To which the father confessed, "I believe; help my unbelief." There it is—warring twins of belief and unbelief.

Soon Jesus would cast out the demon. He did what even the disciples could not do.

At one time or another, life steps into a milk can and we can't get out. We think of such times: a broken relationship, an enraged daughter, a mentally ill son, a lost job, a besetting sin, a terminal diagnosis, a bond crushed. At times like those, we can't just give up and go home. The disciples might not know what to do, but there is One who knows.

Cling to Jesus. Have faith. He will not send you away.

Pray out loud

What is the need you bring to Jesus? Tell him that need and pray, "I believe; help my unbelief."

For further reading: Mark 9:14-24.

5

Being Goliath

Everybody knows we're to "suffer the little children" (Mark 10:14, KJV). Sometimes we need some help.

Like when David and Goliath showed up in our curriculum. I didn't want a fabric storyboard or a video Goliath. I sent my printer friend Victor a giant image. "Can you make the biggest one ever?" I texted. It was Saturday night. Probably not on such short notice.

Sunday morning, Victor found me and asked, "Where do you want Goliath?" He brought it our way. Oh my! That was bigger than I imagined.

I walked to our room with Goliath. It was early enough that not too many people saw me. It's hard to be inconspicuous when there's an almost-life-size Goliath under your arm.

Lorraine started the story with Samuel anointing David as king and then came the Philistines.

Victor had made an opening in the head where I could put my face and talk to the kids from high up in the room. I stood on the piano bench; the two-dimensional Goliath was a sort of shield between me and the kids.

I issued Goliath's challenge to the young Israelites. It's easy to talk big. Now was my chance to let out some roars.

I could see the effect on them. Who would fight such a big man? They looked around. We explained that the real-life Goliath was even bigger than the one we had.

Then Goliath began to make fun of these little people. "I would squash whoever they brought forward. Stomp on him like he was an ant." It was surprisingly easy to get into character. And not just for me—some of the boys laughed; girls too. Stomping ants can be fun.

Then little David stepped forward.

His brothers looked away. Others looked down on him. And Saul—well, his armor wouldn't even fit David.

I looked, through the hole in Goliath's head, down at the children. Each of them was looking up with a certain amount of wonder. And David was looking up in a sweet certainty.

"So you just want to send a little guy like this to fight me?" I bellowed out a laugh-roar.

Again, the kids laughed nervously. Even though we were having fun, Lorraine explained how terrifying it was when it really happened.

We made makeshift stones out of tissue and white labels. David put his hand in his bag, took out a stone and slung it. With another teacher's help, the paper stone struck the Philistine on his forehead. Goliath fell on his face to the ground. The kids cheered and almost danced.

It wasn't the stone but God himself who brought down Goliath.

Kids, bring on the Jesus cheer. God's Word is best enjoyed with little ones. Teachers, learn from students. Listen to them. See Jesus in them. Let all ages celebrate him together.

All things new

Bring on the Jesus cheer. Look for God's fingerprint on your day and then draw or write it.

For further reading: Matthew 19:13-14.

6

Salts of the Earth

As the Lord Jesus said, salt is good, but it needs to keep its flavor (Mark 9:50). Jesus warned us not to lose our saltiness. Salt of the earth staves off rot and keeps the world from going bad. Maybe we are even called to be the salt that stings a wound but helps it heal. Ouch! That hurt, but it's going to be good for me in the long run.

Like varied types, colors and grains of salt, so are the people of God. Indulge me and let's go some different directions.

Table salt is the salt we've all grown up with. It's always there in the cupboard, waiting to be noticed.

One man I know feels most comfortable with the down and out, with the mentally ill. He has the ability to understand and care for them. He points them to Jesus when he can. He sees God's Creator-hand on them. Salt goes to the common places.

Kosher salt is what I use when I want to turn cucumbers into pickles.

Another man I know visits men in jails and tells them about Jesus and the way he can turn shattered hearts into new creations.

Himalayan salt is pink and saltier than regular table salt; we have a lamp made from it. You can pay to sit in a room where the walls are lined with it.

Another friend had hip replacement surgery. The day afterward, she climbed up the stairs of her home without passing out. That was all she could do that day. The next day, God gave her the strength to help set up our church art gallery.

Grey salt, or Celtic sea salt, is thought to help with blood pressure. I'm not sure if I believe it.

One of our disability students writes out a book of the Bible by hand. A whole book. If he makes a mistake, he starts over from the beginning. What a refreshing interaction with God's Word.

Flake salt is big and crunchy, an especially welcome addition to a salad or a sweet where a pinch of salt and texture might add another dimension.

One missionary friend wrote this week to say that some of his colleagues are fleeing or trapped in areas with active airstrikes from fighter jets and regular artillery shelling. One city is seeing particularly heavy fighting, but the situation around the country is changing daily.

I don't know what to say about fleur de sel (flower of the salt). Harvested from the ocean, it's the ultimate flake salt. For most of us, salt is salt, but this one is a finishing salt. When sprinkled on a cookie or a cooked egg, it brings its own flavor to the food.

So many salts, such a big world. May God bless each of us and use us all today.

Crossroad

Present at creation, Jesus knows his salt. He wants to shake us out to flavor the world. How do you flavor the world with grace and truth?

For further reading: Matthew 5:13-16.

7

Gawking at the Rich

Woodward Avenue ran from the Detroit River to the northern suburbs. As you drove out of the city, storefront businesses and car dealerships gave way to high-end restaurants and shops where we went to gawk at the rich. We gawked at big houses, manicured lawns, but sadly no people.

Later in life, I expanded my gawking from the Great Lake State to the Golden State with Malibu, Palm Springs and Beverly Hills. But still there were no rich people outside their homes to gawk at.

The Gospel writers introduce us to two rich people who were different from everyone else. First is the rich ruler in Mark 10. He asks Jesus the right question: "Good Teacher, what must I do to inherit eternal life?" (v. 17). He isn't happy with Jesus' answer to sell all he has, give it to the poor, have treasure in heaven and follow him.

When the people heard Jesus' camel-through-the-eye-of-a-needle comparison, they were caught off guard. He's rich, right? Shouldn't he have a different way to inherit eternal life? Perhaps they gawked at the ruler as he walked away, very sad.

In Luke 19, we meet Zacchaeus—a tax collector who was rich at the expense of others. I wonder if he was glad for the anonymity the Jericho crowd offered. He easily slipped ahead, climbed that sycamore tree to make sure he saw Jesus from *his* vantage point, and remained unnoticed.

Except by Jesus. He not only focused on Zacchaeus but also invited himself over to the tax collector's house. Then the people gawked and grumbled—not at the rich, but at Jesus who had the habit of dining with sinners and other tax collectors, even inviting them to follow him, as Mark described in Mark 2:13-15.

We are not privy to the conversation Jesus and Zacchaeus had, but Luke lets us in on the end of Jesus' visit when the lost Zacchaeus was found and began to store treasures in heaven. Half of my wealth? Sure, why not? Fourfold restitution? No worries. By now, I suspect, the crowd was gawking at both him and Jesus.

Spiritually poor Zacchaeus was now rich, just as we are. In a grand fireworks display of words, Scripture describes God as abounding in steadfast love and compassion, preparing feasts before enemies, lavishing mercy on us, giving us immeasurable riches and a glorious inheritance.

All things new

What would happen if we shared these riches of grace and mercy with someone more like sycamore-tree-climbing Zacchaeus than a respectable rich ruler? What if we caught up with Jesus and said, "Wait, I'm joining you and Zacchaeus for supper." Or if we showed fourfold compassion to the hurting or hurtful. Or we no longer remained absent, and stepped out the front doors, daring to act and speak for all to see, even gawkers like I used to be.

People, behold what God has done. Our gawking will turn to gazing in awe at our Father in heaven.

For further reading: Mark 2:15-17.

8

Glorious Architecture

We enjoy watching Geoffrey Baer on our local television station. He profiles Chicago people, histories and architecture. There have been times when Geoffrey talks about a building I've walked by but never bothered to stop and just look up at, in all its beauty.

I love the Tribune Tower. Its Gothic-cathedral architecture was transposed in the early twentieth century onto a building dedicated to journalism. It's fun to walk around the perimeter and see a bit of architecture from other states and countries.

The Chicago Cultural Center is another easy miss. It's easy to walk by clueless to what's inside. But if you take the time to walk into the building, you won't be disappointed with the magnificent glass and tile and woodwork.

Chicagoans are proud of their city. If someone said they were going to destroy one of the city's landmarks and build it over again in three days, people would call the police to make an arrest.

The Jewish people of Jesus' time were proud of Jerusalem's temple. By all accounts, it was a sight to behold; if you were a person of faith, it was, I'm sure, breathtaking.

Imagine how Jesus' words fell on those who heard them for the first time. When Jesus said that he would destroy the temple and raise it up again in three days, he was speaking to people who didn't have any idea what he was talking about. Some people thought it was a statement worthy of death, which was right—just not in the way they meant it. Quite the opposite.

In his own times, Jesus' power was impossible to miss, but easy to misunderstand.

The temple Jesus referred to wasn't the building, magnificent as it was. And it turned out to be true that the physical temple would be destroyed. But the deeper and truer temple was first the body of Jesus and second the people of God.

Jesus kept telling his followers that he was going to have to die and be raised. They didn't get it. No one wanted to think of Jesus, the wonderful teacher, in this way. They could have embraced him as a liberator from Rome, or the smack-talking truth speaker who put the Pharisees and Sadducees in their place. But dying? No. Let's talk about something else. If I had been there, I would have changed the subject to revisit one of the recent miracles or parables.

When we follow Jesus, we run the risk of facing our own destruction. The Apostles gave their lives for the gospel. People throughout history and even today are paying heavy prices to follow him.

Since the fall, life is marked by violence, strife and death. However, when Jesus, the Creator, died, he brought life to his people—peace, love, hope, life that lasts forever.

Pray out loud

Lord, I want to bring your lasting life to people who are dying, even if it means losing my own, because then I will find it. Amen.

For further reading: John 2:18-22.

9

Royal Sisterhood

We were the ruling royalty of the South Kenwood Avenue kingdom—though that only extended to one block and we were self-crowned. Nonetheless, my sisters and I were benevolent monarchs, gently cajoling our friends to play all games by all our made-up rules.

The finest display of our grandeur was our annual summer backyard plays—written, produced and starring the Royal Sisterhood. We managed our promotion, plastering telephone poles with hand-drawn fliers about the performance. Loyal subjects—uh, neighbors—would come in droves to watch us.

One summer we noticed a decline in the number of subjects in attendance. It turned out that a competing kingdom moved in one block over from ours. It was ruled by Pamela. The call to arms came when we discovered that she was going to put on a play.

We spent the rest of the summer spying on her. We would climb the tree in the backyard for a clear view into Pamela's yard. Better yet was our friend "Tuffy" who remained loyal and lived right next door to Pamela. We would pretend to swim in his pool while keeping a watchful eye on her. We neglected our kingdom and our play planning. We sabotaged her publicity and tore her fliers off telephone poles.

We drove ourselves (and our mother) crazy with this insane need to compare ourselves with Pamela and always come out on top. No, we didn't want to put on a play with her, the Royal Sisterhood decreed. We would rather die than befriend her.

Even Jesus' disciples played the comparison game when they "argued with one another about who was the greatest" (see Mark 9:33-37). When Jesus asked them what they were arguing about, their silence was telling. I know mine would be. Would I really say to Jesus, "Oh, just spying on Pamela to make sure we were still the greatest"?

Even now, I can happily play the comparison game. I don't tear down fliers from telephone poles anymore, but it's hard to avoid comparing homes, children, achievements, social media posts. We even compare how crazy busy we are.

In his book *Mere Christianity* C.S. Lewis wrote: "It is comparison that makes you proud: the pleasure of being above the rest."[2]

The fatal blow to my pride is the recognition that compared to Jesus, I am the inferior one—not Pamela. Any attempt to make myself better than I am will always fall short of his glory. And there, in all my inferiority and otherness, I recollect the amazingly grace-filled words of Ephesians 2:4-5: "But God, being rich in mercy, because of the great love with which he loved us, even when we were dead in our trespasses, made us alive together with Christ—by grace you have been saved..."

It's time to stop playing my favorite game.

Crossroad

Do you have a Pamela in your life? How can God's grace change your attitude toward them?

For further reading: Mark 9:33-34; Philippians 2:1-11.

10

One Less Virtuous Life

In a neighborhood filled with houses of two-parent families and stay-at-home moms, and kids who roamed the streets like free-range chickens, Justine stood out. She lived two doors down from us, with no husband, no kids, no pets. Just Justine. She was the only adult we were allowed to address by first name. We didn't call her Miss Justine or Aunt Justine, and apparently, she had no last name; otherwise, we would have used that.

From our childish perspective, Justine's biggest fault was her choice of Halloween candy. It was so awful that we just stopped going to her front door altogether. The neighborhood band of mothers explained that Justine was frugal and didn't want to waste money on candy for a bunch of clowns. She was also frugal with her time and didn't waste it chatting with the neighbors. If you passed by her house when she was outside, she'd give a curt nod and carry on with whatever she was doing. It was hard to miss the leave-me-be vibes Justine gave off.

Justine could have had her Ebenezer Scrooge moment and stuffed our trick or treat bags with the finest chocolate in town or thrown the best block party ever, but she didn't. She remained aloof and detached, even when my parents and the neighbors mowed her lawn, shoveled her snowy driveway or repaired her car. They were generous and kind to Justine because they had experienced God's generosity.

A lot of us think of frugality as a virtue. We're stewarding our resources, taking care of our families, being wise in our spending, showing tough love, not turning our country into a welfare state. The problem with thinking of frugality and its cousin parsimony as virtues comes when we become economic in our use of resources—such as generosity, compassion, love, kindness and gentleness—and in deciding who should be on the receiving end of them.

The very, very good news is that God is not frugal in his resources. His own words express his extravagant nature. In Genesis 22:17, God doesn't just say that Abraham will have a lot of offspring, but that God will "multiply your offspring as the stars of heaven and as the sand that is on the seashore." God doesn't promise Moses just some land, but a promised land flowing with milk and honey. The psalmists could have written that God is love, instead they wrote that God abounds in love; that he not only removes sins but also removes them as far as the east is from the west.

Frugality isn't a virtue, especially for people upon whom God has lavished the riches of his glorious grace. The true virtue, the true goodness, is when we are like our extravagant God and share with a hurting, dying world his abounding love and mercy that removes their sins as far as the east is from the west.

All things new

Spend five minutes looking at God's extravagant creation; then consider the wonder of his abounding love.

For further reading: Psalm 108:1-4.

11

A Morning Walk with My Dog

When I walk my dog, I have one route in the morning and one in the afternoon. One summer morning, though, we did the afternoon route, and I couldn't help but notice the following scene playing out in one of the driveways.

A young man approached a truck in the driveway, lunch bag in hand, about to leave for the day. Behind him an older man and woman followed him to the truck. There were hugs and words exchanged. The couple watched as he backed the truck out of the driveway and turned down the street. I wondered if he had been visiting and was leaving. Perhaps it was his first day at a new job and his parents were wishing him well, even praying for him. There was something tender in that special moment.

But then we walked on that street another morning, and there they were, hugging, talking, driving away. Whenever else I would walk the dog that way in the morning, there were the three of them. I started to feel like an intruder, so I stopped going that way.

On the first day of school, you see a similar picture, with kids either getting into cars or at bus stops, saying goodbyes. The beginning of school also is the beginning of another year of Sunday school for us. On the first Sunday, there will be comparable scenes for the youngest: a child holding

Mom's or Dad's hands, then parents letting go as the children come into the classroom.

One school year, we had a Palm Sunday lesson in the fall. Teaching it out of season made the truth of it stand out in a fresh way. As I saw people waving to their loved ones, I thought of the people waving palm branches and throwing down their cloaks as Jesus rode by. We long for hope and change, not the promise of a new school year, but instead, a new way of life and a better way to live. Hosanna! Jesus, save us.

Everybody needs rescuing. Jesus performed miracles and then he went to the cross, the grave, the sky. Hallelujah. We are citizens of the heavenly kingdom. Yet for now we live and work in this earthly one. So we walk out to the truck or into the classroom and say goodbye for the day.

Pray out loud

Jesus, help us, as citizens of the heavenly kingdom, to point people to you. Hosanna. Save now.

For further reading: Philippians 3:20-21.

12

Parade of Faith

Communication networks in the time of Jesus were not as sophisticated as our media, social platforms and digital outlets. Yet word got around. Quickly.

Jesus—the man who raised Lazarus from the dead, the one who fed thousands multiple times—he's coming here, to Jerusalem.

And so, the crowd unfolded and grew. Palm branches waving. Coats thrown on the ground in a frenzied worship. And yet it was not as they imagined—they saw a humble man, riding on a donkey.

This parade of faith rides on through history—from the early church to the present day.

Perpetua, a pregnant slave in second-century Rome, had come to faith in Jesus and was sentenced to death, but the spectacle of her execution was delayed due to her pregnancy. After she gave birth to her child, she was paraded into the Coliseum with two other women of faith also condemned to death. Before her execution, guards asked her about being killed so soon after the birth of her only child. She answered: "When I face the beasts there will be another who lives in me, and will suffer for me since I will be suffering for him."

In 1555, John Rogers was paraded to his place of execution. Though he petitioned for chances to visit with family members during his incarceration, such requests were rejected. His children were among the crowd as they followed him to the place of death. Here is part of the exchange he had with his executioner:

"Will you revoke your evil opinions of the Sacrament?"

"That which I have preached I will seal with my blood."

"You are a heretic then."

"That shall be known at the day of judgment."

"I will never pray for you."

"But I will pray for you," Rogers answered, just moments before he was engulfed by flames.[3]

Cole Richards of The Voice of the Martyrs offers this word of perseverance in our modern day: "We must never rest as long as lost people in restricted nations … remain hopeless, without access to the truth that we have in abundance. And we must persevere until every Christian in a restricted nation has a Bible."

Let us live in sacrifice and service in our parade of faith through time.

All things new

Learn about the global persecuted church. Open Doors, Barnabas Aid, Global Christian Relief and The Voice of the Martyrs are good sources.

For further reading: Hebrews 12:1-2.

13

Anonymous, Unknown, Forgotten

With young children, I find that they love to volunteer. If Lorraine or I say, "I need four volunteers," immediately twelve or more hands shoot into the air. Pick me! Adults are not so eager. We adults might wait to see the details of the need before we volunteer. Not true for six-year-olds. They are hungry to help no matter what.

Perhaps it is because I have spent much of my professional life behind the scenes, but there's something special when nameless or forgotten people advance the narrative of the Bible. Or life for that matter. When it happens, it's usually for good.

At other times in the Bible, we are given the names of individuals, but the narrative shows these people surprised by what God has planned for them. When Samuel was looking for the next king, he didn't say he wanted David. He came to Jesse's house and was presented with everyone but the handsome youngest one who was out in the fields with the sheep and his harp—the family forgot him until all others were tried. Even then Samuel had to prompt them. Everyone, even David, was oblivious to a different and better future.

There are many nameless people in the Bible. Psalm writers other than David or Asaph. The woman with the flow of blood. The woman with the alabaster flask. The thief who died next to Jesus. The soldier who pierced Jesus' side. The centurion who confessed. No names are recorded, yet their writing or actions make it into the Bible for us to read about all these years later.

Or think of this example: "Go into the city, and a man carrying a jar of water will meet you. Follow him ..." (Mark 14:13). He was probably the only man carrying a jar of water, at least on that day—though plenty of women were doing that menial but necessary job. So they followed him. The man leads them to where Jesus and the disciples will hold their Passover meal and where Jesus will wash the feet of the disciples and institute the The Lord's Supper.

Can you think of something you do for another person or group where you don't get recognized? You do it anonymously, in secret. Or it's behind the scenes, so no one will know—or if they do, the task is so menial they'll forget.

God sees those kinds of things. Often, people do not see or value them.

Not all children who raise their hands get picked to help out. There are more hands raised than helpers needed. But God's use of people has no such restrictions. When we raise our hands willingly to the Lord, he always has something we can do. We are only limited by our own preoccupations, habits, pride or willingness.

All things new

If we are willing, Jesus can use us in his story. Let's put jars of water on our heads and see where he takes us.

For further reading: Mark 14:1-2; 12-16.

14

Made by Hand

I recently read an article called "Make Something with Your Hands (Even if It's Hideous)." In it, writer Jancee Dunn suggests that making something by hand is good for us. Such activity lowers stress and boosts happiness. The article goes on to say that the act of making can be healing and healthy for the maker.[4]

Something special happens when making and giving combine. A gift that's baked or grown or painted or cooked feels especially personal. It's not the same as ordering a gift from Amazon and having it shipped. Any gift should be appreciated, but handmade makes a difference.

Amazon doesn't carry Julia's Ukraine votives. When Russia invaded Ukraine, Julia brought yellow and blue votive holders to our small group for us to take home, a handmade reminder to pray.

Or Kathryn's cards. She designs a card for any occasion—birthday, Christmas, thank you, many others.

Jesus is creative in and well beyond our creativity, and Jesus was always giving: wine where there was water; fish for empty nets; healing for disease; the ability to walk on water instead of drowning in it; words of truth that have stood the test of time and changed the world for good. When Jesus' hour came, he had made everything: the garden; the torches; the ear he healed; the nails; the wood; even the grave.

Jesus calmed storms, cast out demons, stopped the bleeding. He invited Thomas to touch his wounds, to feel and know the gift of his broken body. Jesus cooked breakfast on the beach. His hands held and hold all—from the foundations of the world to the darkest corner of my heart to the foundations of our faith.

God shaped dust into human form and breathed life into it. Our bodies—every one of them made by God—in many ways have remarkable healing powers built right in. I think sometimes I'm just renting this house I'm living in.

Then with blood and nails and death, God creates something new, but not just a thing. In giving away everything, even life itself, his Son makes a people.

The work of our hands echoes in microscopic ways what Jesus has done and is doing. He incarnated to become one of us. He gave people tasks—drop your nets on the other side of the boat; fill the jars with water; take the boy's lunch and share it. Then he died, rose and ascended—his whole life was a kind of gift. The coming of the Spirit, yet another gift, gives us even more ways to serve one another and the people around us, prompting people to go and share the good news.

We receive. We make. We give away.

Love, the genuine and eternal kind, is made by hands—his and ours.

All things new

Make something with your hands and give it away.

For further reading: Isaiah 66:1-2.

15

Best in Show

Blame it on jet lag, but we were mesmerized with the dog show competition on British TV. I found myself cheering for the underdog, a golden retriever named Taffy. In one relay, the dogs had to pick up a raw egg and carry it from one spot to the other. Taffy dropped her egg. In another relay, the dogs were to carry a hot dog in their mouths to one end of the course and back again. The commentator was clearly upset with my Taffy: "Oh, my. Oh, dear. Taffy just ate the hot dog. She ate the hot dog."

And there sat Taffy, happily licking her lips, unperturbed.

Each dog started with a perfect score. Points were deducted for every wrong action. Taffy was at the bottom.

I thought of Taffy the other day when *The New York Times* reported that "Buddy Holly, a fetchingly bewhiskered petit basset griffon Vendéen, won best in show at the Westminster Kennel Club Dog Show on Tuesday night, beating back a field of fellow champions that included last year's runner-up, Winston the French bulldog."[5]

Apparently, Buddy Holly's owner and trainer had dreamed of this day since she was nine years old.

That dream of being best in the show lives on for a lot of us, well past our ninth birthday. We spend years training for it—we attend the best schools to secure the best careers so we can live in the best neighborhoods and send our children to the best schools. We want to be the best in our lives and the world is the show.

Schools, careers and neighborhoods aren't the real problem.

The problem is the way I size up my competition. Who's the biggest threat to my comfort? Who makes me look good? And who won't? Maybe we should spend less time comparing ourselves with each other.

In Mark 12:38-40, Jesus warned about scribes who like to "have the best seats in the synagogues and the places of honor at feasts, who devour widows' houses and for a pretense make long prayers." This quest for the best was pretense and was no measure of what really counts. Truth is, I'm more like Taffy than Buddy Holly.

The bigger truth is that none of this redeems us or exalts us in God's eyes. Instead of long prayers and devouring others, we need to say every day, "God, be merciful to me, a sinner." He gives grace to the humble, exalting them to the ultimate best in show in heaven and on earth—not on the basis of anything they've done at all. It's all Jesus.

The prize of life is Jesus himself, not accolades or ribbons or trophies.

Crossroad

Form a new habit by praying this every morning out loud: God, be merciful to me, a sinner.

For further reading: Luke 18:9-14.

16

The Widow's Mite

"Jesus sat down near the collection box in the temple and watched as the crowds dropped in their money. Many rich people put in large amounts. Then a poor widow came and dropped in two small coins. Jesus called his disciples to him and said, 'I tell you the truth, this poor widow has given more than all the others who are making contributions. For they gave a tiny part of their surplus, but she, poor as she is, has given everything she had to live on.'"
(Mark 12:41-44, NLT)

Jesus' observation seems almost absurdly out of step with our world. I mean, what financial planner would tell the widow to give the way Jesus praised her for giving? We don't expect that kind of giving. It isn't wise, not to mention that her two small coins wouldn't get her into members-only events at the temple or get her name engraved on a brick or stone.

What motivated the widow to give her cherished mites? Did she give because of the well-run temple? Because she liked the priests? Because of the beauty of the temple building itself? Or did she give because she knew someone who was even worse off than she was? Had she even been waiting to give until the priests did things the way she thought they ought to be done?

The gospel writer described her as a "poor widow." Two strikes against her. She was the one in need. In just a few years, the Apostles would focus on caring for people like her in the newly born church. And a few years later, the temple would be destroyed.

That widow was no more in step with the giving of her own time than with that of ours. Yet perhaps her greatest need at that moment was what prompted her to give, and it didn't have anything to do with the temple. She needed to give to God.

She wasn't in step with the world she lived in, but she was in step with the heart of God, his generous and sacrificial heart. She came closer to being like Jesus than most of us because she gave everything she had. And Jesus noticed. He notices still.

Crossroad

Jesus sees our hearts holding, hoarding, giving, praying, worrying even as we give. He can see right through the popular rationale about how we don't want to be foolish in our giving. But who besides Jesus would have called that widow anything other than foolish? And how does this work today? Dare we answer such a question with actions that Jesus would praise and others would call foolish?

For further reading: Mark 12:41-44; 1 Timothy 6:17-19.

17

The Missionary's Joy

When we served with a mission organization that had summer camps in Russia, we became acquainted with an elderly retired missionary who attended our church. Every summer, she walked to our mission's office to give her donation rather than mail it in. She gave enough to send one child to camp. This gift was personal, from the heart.

A few years later, I was getting ready to go on a summer camp outreach. She enthusiastically gave again.

She wasn't a widow. She had never been married. As I got to know her, I discovered what an amazing and unrecognized lifetime of service she had given to God. But I had to find that out along the way. She wasn't interested in people knowing how God had used her overseas in some amazing ways. And here she was, this time, giving her gift to me, not the mission.

There are many reasons to give or not to give. But the spirit of the widow Jesus praised and this missionary who befriended me amazes me.

The widow Jesus praised wasn't a parable. She was a real person. She gave real money. She would be someone we would say can't afford to give, but it wasn't the institution she was giving to at all. Her gift was for the God of all things, her Maker, Creator, Redeemer and Friend.

The missionary lady moved people. I still think of her. She had such joy when she gave away her money. And that doesn't even get at her faithful prayer support for us and many others.

I don't think they teach this in seminary, but Jesus didn't shy away from it.

The rich young ruler went away sad because of Jesus' admonition to give his wealth away to the poor. Judas, the keeper of the money, thought the alabaster jar should have been sold and given away to the poor. He judged it a terrible waste to pour it out on Jesus—the one who would pay the ultimate price and give more than any of us ever will.

There's something about the way the widow and the elderly missionary lived that doesn't make sense. Yet their examples cry out "Yes" from a different place than we naturally know.

Like a master washing the feet of his servants.

Like thousands eating lunch from one boy's bread and fish.

Or like the empty net cast on the other side, filling with so many fish that it breaks.

Most out of step of all is the King of heaven leaving to be born in a manger, to die forsaken and alone, with some of the last words spilling out of his mouth like the blood from his side being, "Forgive them."

Pray out loud

Jesus, help us break our personal alabaster jars, pouring them out in worship—not looking at others, only gazing at you. All for you, sweet carpenter, fisher of people, gentle Shepherd, Master, Friend.

For further reading: Ephesians 5:1-2.

18

Fire Dependent

Any memories I have of Yellowstone National Park were contained in my View-Master, a childhood toy that made use of small high-quality photographic color images. Thanks to the show *Aerial America* on the Smithsonian Channel, my view of Yellowstone expanded.[6]

On one episode, the camera flew over forests of Lodgepole pines, then cut to footage from devastating wildfires in 1988. The pine trees had become black charred sticks and littered close to 800,000 acres. So how did the new Lodgepole pines grow? Was there a massive campaign to plant them?

The narrator explained a remarkable trait of these pines—the intense heat of the wildfires opened the trees' cones, releasing thousands of new seeds that brought "new life" to the forests. The Lodgepole pines are a "fire-dependent" species.

I am not such a species. I am "fire-averse" when it comes to trials of the fiery kind that lie in my pathway. My first reaction is usually one of surprise. How did this happen? This trial wasn't supposed to be part of God's plan for my wonderful life. My plan included more comfort and ease than hardships and anxious thoughts.

My second reaction is practical. How do I maneuver around the trial? What can I fix to make everything right? I want to hurry to the other side of the trial, with a happy ending of how great everything turned out.

Peter and James were Lodgepole pines—made fire dependent from being with Jesus. In Peter's letter to the early church, he echoes Jesus' warning in Mark 13 that his followers would be beaten and brought to trial: "Beloved, do not be surprised at the fiery trial when it comes upon you to test you, as though something strange were happening to you" (1 Pet. 4:12).

James took Jesus' promise in Mark 13:13 to heart that "the one who endures to the end will be saved," writing: "Blessed is the man who remains steadfast under trial, for when he has stood the test he will receive the crown of life, which God has promised to those who love him" (James 1:12).

Peter and James knew that the intense heat of trials would explode into revealed glory and crowns of life in the presence of Jesus. New life bursts out of heat and fire. It was true for those first-century Christians. It is true for Christians in China, North Korea, Pakistan and Nigeria. Reluctantly, it has to be true for me too.

That trial of the fiery kind? It's still in my pathway, but today, I inched a bit closer to its heat, singing softly:

> "When through fiery trials your pathway shall lie,
> my grace, all sufficient, shall be your supply;
> The flames shall not hurt you. I only design
> your dross to consume, and your gold to refine."[7]

Pray out loud

Pray or sing the hymn "How Firm a Foundation" in your fiery trials.

For further reading: James 1:2–4.

19

Ashes on Beauty

Aunt Kay and Uncle Don were fixtures of my childhood. Their Christian counterparts were Uncle John and Aunt Betty. Neither couple were actual family, but family formed from community.

During the summer, before the dads came home from work, Aunt Kay would walk across the street to our house, cigarette in hand, to join my mother on the front porch for neighborhood gossip. But first, my mom would instruct us to get an ash tray for Aunt Kay.

We didn't own ash trays. What my mother was asking was for us to choose the prettiest teacup from her small but treasured collection, and bring its saucer out for Aunt Kay—you guessed it—to tap her cigarette ashes into. Disgusting.

By far the prettiest teacups were from Aunt Betty, who would bring back a cup and saucer from her trips to Scotland to visit her family. We would purposely choose one of Aunt Betty's cups, hoping our mother would ask us to put it back—they were too perfect, too much of a treasure for butts and ashes.

Nope. We were indignant at my mother's careless attitude toward her fine china. What prompted our indignation was that the teacups were off-limits for our al fresco parties. Mother did not want us to ruin her lovely teacups with mud and sticks. Really, Mom? It was okay for Aunt Kay to ruin them? My pharisaical leanings were already showing, even at such a young age.

Jesus had a similar careless attitude, not to fine china but to alabaster flasks. The disciples knew better. In Mark 14—sandwiched between the chief priests and scribes plotting to kill Jesus, and Judas Iscariot's betrayal—we see Jesus, not on a porch, but at a table in the house of Simon the leper. Then a woman walks into the room, breaks an expensive alabaster jar and pours the oil on Jesus' head.

Talk about the indignation flying around that table—why did the woman waste the ointment? Why did she ruin the flask? They could have sold it all to give to the poor. Mark says that they scolded her.

Then Jesus says, "Leave her alone. Why do you trouble her? She has done a beautiful thing to me" (v. 6). Her act of ruin became a gospel proclamation as she anointed Jesus' body beforehand for burial, and beauty would come from the ashes of betrayal and death.

We adored Aunt Betty, but my mother knew her better than we did. She would not have minded the burning cigarette finding rest on her bone china gift. In fact, if she were on that porch, she probably would have made for Aunt Kay Scottish cream scones and served tea in the now saucer-less cup, as my mom dumped the ashes in a beautiful display of grace.

Ashes on beauty, beauty for ashes.

Crossroad

What ashes of sin do you need to give to Jesus in exchange for his beautiful grace?

For further reading: Mark 14:3–9.

20

Playground Church

My school was Garfield Elementary. St Lucy's was where the children next door went. They were Spanish-speaking Roman Catholics. I was Baptist. I knew there were differences. Between 3:00 and 5:00, those differences didn't matter. It was time to play. One day we decided to play church.

They ran inside their house to get a book that wasn't a Bible, a chrome cross with Jesus hanging on it, a bag of confetti, trinkets and a goblet.

"Let's do a wedding," Deborah announced.

Mary and Miguel would be bride and groom. I was priest. The procession started. I looked at Miguel and wondered if we shouldn't have ditched the girls and found some guys for a ballgame. Too late.

Suddenly the wedding turned into communion. This happened once a month at my church, never at weddings.

Deborah explained that they did it all the time. She filled the goblet with water and drops of red dye. What I thought was confetti turned out to be communion wafers.

I did not like this. I protested, "This isn't right. Those are for church." She got frustrated and declared a snack break.

They offered some of the wafers as a snack. "It's okay," they said. "They haven't been blessed yet."

I had no idea what that meant. I looked at the little tissue-paper-thin circles. I put one in my mouth and it instantly dissolved.

"Take more," Deborah said. "One isn't enough for a real snack."

They explained how the wafers were nothing special until the priest blessed them. Before that, they were just any food. After that, we couldn't eat them.

Real food for me was peanut butter and bread, not something made for communion, Catholic or Protestant. Suddenly their mom looked out at the Catholic items transfigured into toys and shouted, "What are you doing?" and more in Spanish. They ran inside.

Later I asked my mom how the priest could change the wafer into something more than food. "Catholics believe that when the priest blesses the wafer, it turns into Jesus," she explained. "We don't believe that."

I didn't want to play church anymore. It didn't matter if it was blessed by a priest or not. I felt guilty eating from that bag.

The good news for my guilt was that Jesus did break bread and did drink from the cup. It was no play but reality. Jesus' body was broken, his blood poured out, and my sins—our sins, the sins of the world—were washed away.

All things new

Something special happens at the Lord's Table. It's not a game. I don't do it alone, but with the family of God. It's looking not only back, but also ahead to a wedding in the future. Memorize these true words of God in Revelation 19:9: "And the angel said to me, 'Write this: Blessed are those who are invited to the marriage supper of the Lamb.' And he said to me, 'These are the true words of God.'"

For further reading: Revelation 19:6–9.

21

Is It I?

Previous debates of who was the greatest, asking who could sit on the right and left sides of Jesus enthroned, evaporated during dinner when Jesus said that one of them would betray him. He had, after all, just washed their feet.

Jesus was always serving. Now he had cleaned other people's feet. Did they remember John the Baptist saying he wasn't worthy to loosen the straps of his sandals?

The occasionally courageous followers lost their appetites. "They began to be sorrowful and to say to him one after another, 'Is it I?'" (Mark 14:19). He said it, so it must be true. I wonder how many of them prayed, "No, not me. Please."

These little followers would become our church fathers, but not yet.

They were accustomed to believing and following what Jesus said, but that Last Supper night was different. Jesus had spoken. There was one who would betray and everyone would scatter.

This was before there were Christians for Saul to hate, while Stephen still lived. Their minds had readily wondered who would be sitting closest to Jesus when he would reign, but on that night one question was heavy in the air: Is it I?

After all they'd been through together, what kind of love turns its back on the Master?

What kind of love forsakes a heavenly throne for an earthly manger?

What kind of love denies the Master they've left their nets to follow?

What life only loves from humblest birth to horrific death?

We are asked, like Peter warming himself at the fire, aren't you one of his followers?

The science teacher who asked out of the blue if you believe in God.

The neighbor who pulled back when he realized how often you go to church.

A work friend at coffee break reading the Koran.

The man who brings milk to your door or mail to your box.

The parent, child, sibling, cousin, grandchild, godparent, friend from ages past.

Real love is unknown to any of us save Jesus. Here is the only love story that has ever been. The story lives in me but is his, not mine. We can only sing a song of love because our water becomes his wine.

It is a foreign story, an alien truth; ours to hold and to carry and tell, but not of us. This is not the story of my love, known or unknown, but the life song of his love freely given.

> "Here might I stay and sing
> No story so divine!
> Never was love, dear King,
> Never was grief like Thine.
> This is my Friend, in whose sweet praise
> I all my days could gladly spend."[8]

All things new

Ask God to give you one opportunity for a gospel conversation with someone you know.

For further reading: Mark 14:18–25.

22

Engraved Invitation

We have been married for many years, but I haven't forgotten the stress of wedding planning. We met weekly to go over the nuts and bolts of the wedding, even hand-addressing the envelopes of our engraved invitations, with reply cards enclosed so people could say if they were coming.

One New York City couple, featured in a bridal magazine, had an invitation list of 350 people.[9] They would get married in a big cathedral, ride around the city in a double-decker bus, stop for photo ops at landmarks, eat a steak and lobster dinner. The cost was about $150,000.

News agencies picked up the story. The couple explained that they needed to winnow the guests from 350 to 60, the number who would fit on the double-decker bus. "It was stressful," the groom said. "We had to figure out a way for them to choose us, because we can't choose them."

This couple's invitation asked each invitee to purchase a ticket to the wedding for $333 apiece. Problem solved: their guest list fell from 350 people invited to 60 who paid. Everyone could fit on the bus.

A wedding is fraught with tensions: relatives, invoices, where to seat different people—the list goes on.

Then the day comes. Something new is born. The church witnesses wonder: two become one.

God's invitation needs no whittling down. His invitation is extravagant, reckless. It's a head-crushing invitation. It can drown an army in a river, close the mouths of ravenous lions, keep people alive in the hottest of furnace fires. It's a man impaled on a spike he fashioned for his enemy. It's the hated brother who all but died rescuing the ones who threw him into a pit to die. It's oasis in drought. It's wine where water belongs. It's words engraved on hearts, a message written on bloodied hands and the side of the groom himself. It's the bride blushing with the realization that the groom longs for her. From betrayed to betrothed, she turns to him and says the words from the Last Supper with a new meaning, "Is it I?" (Mark 14:19).

Oil lamps are filled in anticipation. Yes, come.

Come from secular Manhattan to the prisons of North Korea, to the apartment church under electronic surveillance in China, to the Christian widow in the Middle East whose son and daughter-in-law evicted her from the apartment she gave them—all are turning to Jesus with the blushing, humble, shy beauty of a maiden who senses a love never before cast her way. Looking into his eager eyes, she marvels, "Is it I?"

Yes, it is.

All things new

Look for God's extravagance in the sunrise or sunset, stars and moon.

For further reading: Isaiah 55:1; Revelation 22:17.

23

Garden Tours

I've never met her, but I want Dana Smith as my new best friend. My friend Dana wrote this in *The New York Times* one fine spring day: "Last Saturday, I was covered in dirt, my back ached, the scream of a trillion cicadas rang in my ears, and, despite my best efforts, a sunburn was developing on the back of my neck. I was in heaven."[10]

I am right there with you, new friend. My garden, any garden is heavenly. Dana pointed out what fellow gardeners know—gardening is good for your physical and mental well-being.

There are other gardens that we need to linger in for the sake of our souls.

First is the garden God planted in Eden, where he put the man whom he had formed (see Gen. 2:8). I do wonder about our first parents' gardening skills, or more accurately their listening skills, as this garden became the backdrop for humanity's fall into sin.

English poet John Milton described this fall in the opening lines of *Paradise Lost*:

> "Of Man's First Disobedience, and the Fruit
> Of that Forbidden Tree, whose mortal taste
> Brought Death into the World, and all our woe ..."[11]

In this woe, however, is the promise of other gardens to come. We hear it in "the sound of the LORD God walking in the garden in the cool of the day" (Gen. 3:8), seeking newly lost humanity. We hear it in God's words to the serpent about Eve's offspring: "he shall bruise your head, and you shall bruise his heel" (v. 15). We also see the promise in God's covering of Adam and Eve.

The promise continues in the garden of Gethsemane, against a backdrop of a supper of bread and wine, of betrayal and denial, of sorrow even to death. Scripture's Second Adam does what the first Adam did not do in paradise; in a bleak garden, he says, "Yet not what I will, but what you will" (Mark 14:36). And the blows begin to fall on the serpent's head.

Then comes a garden by a tomb, where one might be excused for looking for a serpent, who perhaps did deliver a fatal blow. But not Mary Magdalene—she was looking for her Savior. And in that beautiful ironic way of Scripture, who should come to her but a gardener, walking in the cool of the morning, calling Mary's name, dispelling any lingering serpents and sending Mary on her way to the disciples.

Crossroad

The last garden is the garden we linger in now, where we pull weeds of jealousy, selfish ambition, boasting and false idols. With wise garden advice, we can sow love, joy, peace, patience, kindness, goodness, faithfulness, gentleness and self-control—reaping a harvest of righteousness until the first Eden gives way and paradise is restored.

For further reading: Genesis 3:8-10; Mark 14:32-36; John 20:14-16.

24

Under the Bus

Two separate stories on my news feed recently claimed that Politician A threw Politician B under the bus. Or was it the other way around? No matter, both politicians are now under the bus, which might be a good thing or not.

As the youngest of three girls, one might think that I would be well acquainted with the underside of a bus, as an easy target for blame whenever our sibling skirmishes got out of hand.

According to the Merriam-Webster dictionary:

> "No one is certain where the phrase 'throw (somebody) under the bus'—meaning to betray or sacrifice a person, particularly for the sake of one's own advancement, or as a means of safe-guarding one's own interests—comes from. But there's probably enough evidence to throw British English under the bus."[12]

Perhaps the venerable dictionary should have looked elsewhere for the origin of this idiom, such as the Garden of Eden. The serpent intentionally threw Adam and Eve under the bus in the first move to advance his kingdom. Adam and Eve may not have been as intentional as the serpent, but they were quick to safeguard their own interests to avoid blame. It's remarkable how much we resemble our first parents in shifting blame, a bit like the advice my car insurance agent always gives—don't admit fault; and if a bus happens to pass by, all the better.

I look at Merriam-Webster again and read the words betrayal and sacrifice. This is the language of a supper of bread and wine shared with a betrayer. It is the language of another garden at another time, where a reputation was not considered a thing to be grasped; where the Son, like his Father in the cool of the day in that first garden, came to seek and save the lost.

It's not in a dictionary, but in God's living Word, where the language of grace and mercy and of rescue and restoration begins to make a miraculous and unfathomable kind of sense. It is there that we see the Stone the builders rejected become the cornerstone of a new way of life. It is there that God himself looks, even goes under the bus, to wherever we've been hiding. Jesus finds us and keeps taking the guilt and blame on himself.

Pray out loud

Thank you, God, that you forgive us and bring us under your rule and kingdom. In that hiding place we find ourselves transformed, a people no longer in darkness but living, working, walking in your marvelous light.

For further reading: Luke 19:1–10.

25

Mistaken Identity

"You look Russian," our missionary friend Cindy said as we exited the Metro station near Red Square. "Just don't smile." It was 1993—the early years of the fall of communism—and we were headed to two protest rallies in Red Square: one pro-communist, one pro-democracy.

"I look Russian and I won't smile," I repeated as we arrived at the pro-communist rally. That woman on the tram spoke to me in Russian. As long as I stayed mute, I could be mistaken for a Russian citizen.

The rally was eerily silent. Protestors were mainly pensioners in dark winter coats and Russian hats. The people stood as if in formation, listening to a lone man shout angrily through a portable speaker.

We walked behind the protestors without a word, headed to the other rally. We passed by Russian soldiers on horseback and Moscow police primed for violence.

"Look," Cindy said, "Lorraine's jacket is the exact color of the new Russian flag." The blue color was not welcome in this all-red rally. So, would they think I was Russian, but the wrong kind of Russian? Thanks, Cindy. I just wanted to get by the soldiers and the armed police. Fine if you mistake me for a Russian citizen.

The pro-democracy rally could not have been more different. No formations or angry screaming speeches. People talked and laughed. Ice-cream vendors sold ice cream. Phew, I could smile and talk again and shake off my mistaken identity, free to be myself.

I think in some ways that same feeling was true at that time for other people coming out of the spell of the Soviet Union. They weren't Communists anymore. They weren't Soviet. Some could finally whisper a confession of identity, like one dear friend who whispered that her mother was a Jew. We hugged because we shared that same heritage with our mothers and shared a bond in Christ. (It's bittersweet to remember this with what's happening between Russia and Ukraine and America, but I'm glad I experienced this.)

The danger with mistaken identities is believing that they are the real deal. There are many ways we create mistaken identities based on externals such as politics, status or success. None of that is who we really are.

Think about the Apostle Peter on what was probably the worst night of his life—his denial of Jesus. Try as he might, there was no mistaken identity for Peter as he huddled around the fire. In Mark 14:66-68, a servant girl reveals Peter's identity: he had been with Jesus.

Crossroad

Being with Jesus defined Peter, even at his lowest point, even when, scared, he denied it. And it is what needs to define us as children of God at our lowest or highest points. Consider how you can let people see you for who you really are—a child of the living God, which is the very best identity that any of us could aspire to.

For further reading: Mark 14:66-72.

26

No Strangers Here

My mom, Grace, knew no strangers. In her later years, she relocated to Jefferson City, Missouri, to be closer to my middle sister and her family. She moved into an apartment building. A little while later, we went to visit her. We had been there for a few minutes when knock, knock.

Grace opens the door. Zona, the lady from downstairs, has brought my mother her house plants to nurse back to health. In she comes. She tells us how much she loves Mom. Zona drinks my mom's coffee over Bible verses, angel food cake, summer fruits.

Knock, knock. Grace opens the door. Bill, the handyman with tattoos on his arms and a handlebar mustache, comes to happily repair her shower head. While she waits for him to finish, she makes his lunch.

Knock, knock, knock, knock. It's Rosie from across the hall. Grace opens the door. Later she explains to us that Rosie "wasn't quite right, but she's okay." Rosie felt free to knock on Mom's door at any time of the day or night. Mom was always there to listen to her fears or dreams or imaginations. Rosie left always feeling loved.

Debbie, a childhood friend from my childhood church, once posted on Facebook how Paul, in Romans 16:1-16, listed name by name people who touched his life. She decided to do the same. The first name she listed?

Grace Lustig, my mother; the second name was another Grace.

These two Graces called themselves "Abundant Grace" and "Amazing Grace." My mother claimed Abundant Grace because of a few extra pounds she had over Amazing Grace.

In some ways it really didn't matter. Both Graces exhibited abundance and amazing grace to rowdy children, to a newly arrived mother from Russia and to a formidable Mrs Mac (whose name also made Debbie's post and would also make my list if I wrote one).

My oldest sister, who lives in Washington D.C. is very much like my mom. She has a knack for collecting people from down the street, in the suburbs and on Capitol Hill—strangers, really, until they enter her home (which is also where her Brethren assembly meets). There, they break bread together—either her homemade bread over a meal or in remembrance of the One who had nowhere to lay his head.

It's in the remembrance of Jesus and his blood spilled and body broken that strangers and aliens become fellow citizens with saints and members of God's household. It's grace that helps us see strangers and aliens as potential family members. It's grace to remember that we, too, were aliens, who needed the same invitation extended to us when we were far off. And it's grace that will bring us home again.

We all could use a visit from grace these days—abundant and amazing.

All things new

Offer food or drink or time to someone who might knock on your door.

For further reading: Ephesians 2:19-21.

27

It's Lonely at the Bottom

I was convinced that I was the only mother at church whose adult child wasn't working or following the Lord or moving into his own apartment. At the Good Friday service, forget contemplating the cross shrouded in black cloth; all I contemplated were happy parents surrounded by happy adult children. It was lonely at the bottom.

According to an essay in *The New York Times*, it turns out that I wasn't special in my loneliness. The essay, titled, "If Loneliness Is an Epidemic, How Do We Treat It?" stated that one-fifth of Americans over eighteen always feel lonely or socially isolated.[13]

Behavioral neuroscientist Dr Stephanie Cacioppo has been moving away from a "pharmaceutical solution" to loneliness and, according to the essay, is "now promoting the acronym [are you ready for this?] GRACE, which stands for 'gratitude, reciprocity, altruism, choice and enjoyment.'"

As Christ followers, GRACE spells out a different solution to a loneliness which is long past the epidemic stage. I suspect it appeared in the beginning when our first parents experienced a break in their relationship with the Creator. And Grace shows up with promises and fig leaves.

Ruth was a swirl of emotions—loneliness probably in the mix—when she threw in her lot with her bitter and lonely mother-in-law. There, Grace shows up in worthy Boaz, turns bitterness to blessing and then enters the kingly line of David.

Even King David wasn't immune to loneliness and despair. In Psalm 6, he languishes; his soul is greatly troubled. He is overwhelmed and exhausted with his moaning and weeping. Grace shows up in the fray with strength and rest.

After 400 years of silence, Grace shows up again, this time in bodily form, as the only Son from the Father. I don't know if this is what Dr Cacioppo had in mind when she suggested that a lonely mind might be healed with help from the body. However, we *are* healed because the Son's body was broken for us, because his wounds brought healing to our souls, because his body was raised.

God's redemptive, healing grace also shows up in a body that thanks God together, that does "nothing from selfish ambition or conceit, but in humility counts others more significant than yourselves" (Phil. 2:3) and looks to the interests of others.

A funny thing happened to me at the bottom of my loneliness. We told our small group about some of the issues with our adult child, and it turned out that everyone in our group had someone they loved with the same issues. Suddenly it was very crowded at the bottom as we cried together, prayed together and made room for Grace—make that more grace. We lifted up each other and found rest in the One who was lifted up for us.

All things new

How has grace shown up in your life?

For further reading: 2 Corinthians 8:8-9.

28

The In-Between Day

On Good Friday we leave church in silence and darkness, but my social posts quickly fill with assurances that Easter is coming.

Jesus' first followers didn't have the luxury of bypassing Saturday. By the time Saturday dawned, their Easter story had been marred by betrayal, bitter tears, despair. The Savior could but didn't come down from the cross to save himself, so his followers watched him breathe his last. Then Joseph of Arimathea went to work quickly and secretly to take away Jesus' body, which he and Nicodemus wrapped in linen and spices—not with resurrection in mind, but because of the Jewish day of preparation.

For some of us, the solemnity of Good Friday quickly gives way on Saturday to Easter's triumphant song:

> "Made like him, like him we rise, Alleluia!
> Ours the cross, the grave, the skies, Alleluia!"[14]

Saturday is the day we get ready for Resurrection Day, in one way or another.

For others of us, ours is still the cross and grave. We relate more to loss and fear than we do to hope and joy. We sit in Saturday's darkness, painfully aware of its suffocating silence and uncertainty. For me, it's the uncertainty that nothing will change for a sick family member. Am I going to be perpetually stuck in this bleak day before Easter?

Some women had followed Jesus and had trailed Joseph of Arimathea to the tomb. Mark 15:46 says they watched Joseph lay Jesus' body just so and then roll a great stone to its entrance. Now they were back again with spices and ointment to lovingly attend to Jesus' corpse.

And Mark lets us in on their conversation: "Who will roll away the stone for us from the entrance of the tomb?" (16:3). How confusing it must have been when there was no stone at the entrance and no dead body to tend.

Imagine burial spices going every which way when they saw an angel of the Lord in the tomb, who greeted them with the understatement of the century: "Do not be alarmed. You seek Jesus of Nazareth, who was crucified. He has risen; he is not here" (Mark 16:6). Saturday's shock and grief gave way to Easter resurrection.

As kids, my sisters and I dubbed large grey clouds with shafts of sunlight beaming through them "Second Coming Clouds." These shafts are called Crepuscular rays—"God rays". The sunbeams originate when the sun is just below the horizon, during twilight hours. God rays are noticeable when the contrast between light and dark is most obvious, like between Easter Saturday and Easter morning.

Pray out loud

Thank you, God, that for all of us who sit in the darkness, ours *is* the cross, the grave, the skies.

For further reading: Psalm 31:21-24.

29

Drowning

I did a lot of odd jobs growing up: cutting lawns for haircuts, painting my trumpet teacher's garage for music lessons. But my first real job was working at the day camp at the YMCA.

When it was time for the children to go into the pool, my job was to make sure none of them drowned. I learned mouth-to-mouth resuscitation, and never had to use it. No one drowned on my watch, but I do remember pulling up a lot of kids who seemed like they had been under too long, their heads breaking the surface of water, laughing, smiling, coughing, mildly choking if they swallowed some chlorinated water.

One day when I was off work, I went to the municipal pool in my city's park. It was nice to swim on my own, no kids to worry about. I swam underwater a full length of the pool. It was great.

Holding my breath, swimming at the bottom of the pool, I didn't hear anything. However, I saw underwater bodies heading to the ladders and the sides, everyone getting out of the water at the same time, except for one pair of legs walking to the side after everyone else had fled. I surfaced and saw a lifeguard with a child in his arms. He was doing mouth to mouth. Everyone stood looking, wanting, hoping to hear the cough, the choke, the catching of breath. Pool staff rushed everyone out of the pool and into the park.

The ambulance came; the child was wheeled out, eyes open, looking very much scared and alive. The pool closed for the rest of the day. You can believe that when I went back to work on Monday, I was more aware than ever of every child entrusted to my care.

Sunday morning, in our Sunday school for youngsters, we get to tell the story of Jesus calming the storm in Mark 4. We make the boat and the storm, and act it out as a whole group. And with all of the waves and the storm going strong, we wake up Jesus.

Help us. We're going to drown. Don't you care?

Real waves. Real fear. An ocean roiling all around us, swallowing us into death.

And then Jesus gets up and says, "Peace! Be still!" (v. 39).

The children all at once are silent (at least it's always worked so far). The storm is stopped. Drowning averted. Faces frozen between fear and fun.

Jesus asks, "Why are you so afraid? Have you still no faith?" (v. 40).

That near drowning at the pool seems like such a long time ago, and yet the memory and the danger still seem fresh.

All things new

The metaphor of drowning extends to the people around us who don't know Jesus—while we might be drowning in tasks or fears or worries, what about people who think they're fine but don't know the storm around us all? What kind of lifeguards are you and I now?

For further reading: Mark 4:35–41.

30

The Forgiveness Project

I read an article in *The New York Times* titled, "Let Go of Your Grudges. They're Doing You No Good."[15] As I read the article, I had a flashback to similar childhood advice we probably all received—don't hold grudges. The author also referenced the Stanford University Forgiveness Project. Decades ago, a foundation donated money for the university to study forgiveness and its psychosocial and physiological benefits. In short, the conclusion: we should forgive others because it's good for us.

That first Stanford University Forgiveness Project led to more projects, books, events and the inevitable website that lists nine steps in forgiving someone. One of the steps states, "Forgiveness is for you and not anyone else."[16]

It's true that bearing a grudge can hold the bearer in debilitating bonds. However, if one of my young children in Sunday school said, "Forgiveness is just for me, not anyone else," I would probably give my handy teacher answer—"Well, I never really thought of that before"—instead of saying, "What are you thinking? Forgiveness is self-centered?"

Grace, my mother, had her own forgiveness project of which my sisters and I were frequent subjects. The project involved either the subjects asking forgiveness for a wrong done, or receiving the apology and forgiving the other subjects involved. In short, my mother's conclusion: we forgive because Christ forgave us.

We have no personal power to change ourselves, let alone forgive anyone, apart from the spotless Lamb of God and his grace. Psalm 103 is not your typical Scripture for Lent, but we would do well to dwell there this season—dwell on our gracious, compassionate, merciful God who forgives all our iniquity, heals all our diseases, and "as far as the east is from the west, so far does he remove our transgressions from us" (v. 12).

Crossroad

Before my mother's forgiveness project, before Stanford University's forgiveness project and before the foundation of the world, God's once-for-all, all-sufficient forgiveness project was in place. Come to Jesus and find his forgiveness and grace.

For further reading: Psalm 103:6-13.

31

Scattered Clothes

My Jewish-turned-Christ-follower mother incorporated a lot of her upbringing in bringing up my sisters and me. Our favorite was no work on the Sabbath, which meant no chores from Saturday evening to Monday morning. Our shared space became a wilderness of unmade beds, homework buried under piles of clothes, shoes out of closets. Our room had to regain order come Monday morning, but that didn't stop us from throwing clothes on the floor.

I thought about my childhood wasteland the other day as I read the Gospel accounts of Jesus' last few weeks on earth. There's a lot of mention about clothes and cloaks on the ground or floor, or in and out of tombs.

There's Lazarus, the dead man who came out of the tomb, hands and feet still wrapped with strips of linen, even though his sister Martha warned everyone of their bad odor. When Jesus instructed those at the tomb to take off his grave clothes, I suspect Lazarus dumped those rotting clothes on the ground without a second thought. Time for some new clothes.

And then there's Jesus. He shrugged off his outer clothing, wrapped a towel around his waist and picked up a basin of water to wash his disciples' feet. In another wardrobe change, Jesus wears a crown of thorns and a purple robe. Oddly enough, he didn't shrug off this robe or crown nor even denounce the cries for his crucifixion.

All this leads to grave clothes again—Jesus' grave clothes. We watch Joseph and Nicodemus—a secret disciple and a night visitor to Jesus—carefully wrap his dead body with strips of linen and seventy-five pounds of myrrh and aloe. Did Joseph weep over the fragrant spices for burial? As Nicodemus prepared this lifeless body for burial, did he recite the Teacher's words to him: "For God so loved the world, that he gave his only Son, that whoever believes in him should not perish but have eternal life" (John 3:16).

Death is a strange way to bring about forgiveness and eternal life.

One dead man is called out of the tomb and lives; one dead man enters the tomb, and we live.

One man is freed from death's stench; the other takes on the stench of sin and death, and exchanges our rot for his righteousness, freeing us from sin's penalty.

A tomb is a strange place to find linen cloths scattered about and a face cloth, for the dead, folded up by itself. Indeed, this empty tomb is a strange place for the fragrance of spices to linger long after three days. The reality of those odors reminds us that Jesus really did die. He put on the clothes of death. But then he took them off and left them on the floor of the tomb for all to see.

Pray out loud

Thank you, God, that the One who was dead is risen, ascended, interceding, living in and with us, now and forevermore.

For further reading: John 20:1–10.

32

Bistro Margosha

Jesus said:

> "Truly, I say to you, there is no one who has left house or brothers or sisters or mother or father or children or lands, for my sake and for the gospel, who will not receive a hundredfold now in this time, houses and brothers and sisters and mothers and children and lands, with persecutions, and in the age to come eternal life. But many who are first will be last, and the last first." (Mark 10:29-31)

Margosha rose early. She didn't have to get to work; work was where she lived. Margosha slept in what was supposed to be a pantry closet in the back of the bistro. That was more than enough for her. Gone were the days of perfumed linens and the dressing table she inherited from her grandmother. She remembered how proud her grandmother had been of the red star jewelry. She used to wonder if it was really made of diamonds or something less. As a child, it had all been real and true. Babushka had been a good Soviet believer.

That was another life. Before the God of love and life came to her, she loved the ways of her grandparents. Then something else found her, and nothing else had any meaning or allure.

When she was released from her prison term, they let her out the front gate. No one greeted her. Margosha fled the city and journeyed into the birch forest to the east. She was already east, but maybe she thought to go even further. This would be the end of everything, and in a sense, it was. Her old life was gone: the wealth and privilege; the dividends to her family loyalty. It was freeing to be done with them.

Now, after tea and a humble Grenki toast, and a moment with the Psalms, Margosha began to prepare the morning porridge, the samovar tea, the vegetables for today's soup.

Pavel didn't know where the bus was to take him but he was glad to be on it, and passed out from exhaustion. He woke as in a daze. The glass window on the bus had formed ice crystals in the winter wilderness. He rubbed it with the sleeve of his jacket to be able to see, but it was hopeless today. Nevertheless he tried to look through it, to pretend that he could see on the other side.

After an hour or so, Pavel stumbled off, acting like he had a place to go. The bus spat him out and moved on. He was awash with fumes and cold, and walked toward the only place whose light welcomed him: Bistro Margosha.

She gave him hot porridge and chai. When he motioned to pay, she glanced at him and began to collect his dishes. "On the house," she said.

He had no words.

All things new

Invite someone you don't typically hang out with to coffee or tea. Find something you have in common.

For further reading: Hebrews 13:1-2; 1 Corinthians 2:9-10.

33

Active Listening

As I told the story of missionary Adoniram Judson and his journey to Burma (now Myanmar) in Sunday school last week, I had some competition. No disrespect to the teacher, but kids had business to conduct with other kids. A missing tooth. A birthday. A new toy. A new baby brother. A biting problem. The need to go potty.

"Wait," I said, looking at the culprits. "We can't all talk at once. It's my turn to talk right now." Three claps of the hands sometimes work.

We teachers act like grown-ups, always listening when they're supposed to. But we're lying.

How many times a day am I halfway there? What was that article I just read? How much is the auto mechanic going to set me back? What's my next meeting? Wait. Someone's talking. Oh, now, what was that you were saying?

No matter how well we act like good listeners in front of the kids, we aren't very good at hearing what other people say.

Jesus kept telling people to listen. Let those with ears hear.

While we have a hard time listening, God never turns a deaf ear to us. I find solace in the truth that God actively listens, knows, always hears. I don't think we really believe that's true. We live like our sin is stronger than God's Son. Ultimately, though, God's listening atones for everything.

Give ear, give ear, I feel the need to complain, to pour out the words of my pre-Easter sadness and pain. I wonder, God, do you hear me? Perhaps I don't even think about you. Do you know and care? Are you there? Even more to the point: if you should answer, do I hear you?

Where can I go that you cannot hear? What words can I think that you do not see? If I wonder where you were when my best friend died, your listening ear is not stopped; it does not hide. Even if I wander down the street of my grand illusion of want, or the anger or shame of my ghostly haunt, still you hear without being called. When I ask the world why, I'm talking to you. Eyes to hear, ears to see.

Into your hands I commit my words. You hear even the words I cannot speak, the ones I don't know I have. With you there is only nearness, sheer nearness; ever and ever, you are here—not over there but right here, closer than my imagination dreams.

Pray out loud

"Incline your ear to me;
  rescue me speedily!
Be a rock of refuge for me,
  a strong fortress to save me!
For you are my rock and my fortress;
  and for your name's sake you lead me and guide me;
you take me out of the net they have hidden for me,
  for you are my refuge."

(Psalm 31:2-4)

For further reading: Psalm 31.

34

Daydreams

"Therefore stay awake—for you do not know when the master of the house will come, in the evening, or at midnight, or when the rooster crows, or in the morning—lest he come suddenly and find you asleep. And what I say to you I say to all: Stay awake." (Mark 13:35-37)

Forgetting is daydreaming and mistaking that for the real thing.

After Jesus fed thousands with a few fish and loaves, the disciples worried about food. It might seem like you have a lot better trust in Jesus than they, but don't be so sure.

Which tomatoes should I buy—heirloom, cherry, beefsteak, plum, on-the-vine, Roma, grape, currant, red, yellow, black?

Screens can put us in dreamland, especially those that flow one episode into the next. Even the best show can get dreamlike as you watch, and hours pass by.

When we value individual beliefs, it's easy to forget that not all our friends know Jesus, even if they are nice, daresay nicer, than some Christians. We can nod off when it comes to being liked and enjoying life with people who don't yet have the taste of eternity we so freely eat. Maybe God wants to use us to bring change and hope—but we need to be willing to put our mouth where our heart is. If we settle for common values with a friend who doesn't know Jesus, we may cheat them out of eternal love. Nothing takes the place of Jesus, no matter how valued it is.

I cherish my books. I love pulling out a book I haven't looked at in years, finding notes in the margin, remembering what was going on when I wrote it. Nostalgia. Or I yearn for the new just-out title.

What about that latest podcast? I'm imagining the next trip—by plane, train or car, and will it be near an ocean? Or a connection with a friend or family, or a museum or gallery or play I've never been to.

I was wondering: How can I squeeze more out of my day? Can I pack more in an hour?

AI means what took two hours now takes two minutes. Some might call it a new efficiency, but it might also be a way to soften the mind and retreat into new daydreams, and what you end up with … is it even you?

Our sleepiness robs us of readiness. Then the rooster crows, jarring us. We, like Peter, hear that crowing wake-up call. The face of Jesus is the face of eternal love, the expression of first love in the first light of day. Look at his beautiful gaze. Watch for him.

Crossroad

What is putting you in dreamland? What do you need to put down or put away to help you see the face of Jesus, and put your mouth where your heart is?

For further reading: Mark 13:35-37; Ephesians 5:13-16.

35

Like My Dog

"Peter said to him, 'Even though they all fall away, I will not.' And Jesus said to him, 'Truly, I tell you, this very night, before the rooster crows twice, you will deny me three times.' But he said emphatically, 'If I must die with you, I will not deny you.' And they all said the same." (Mark 14:29-31)

I need to admit that I am more like the disciples than I am like my dear dog. I am afraid that he loves me more, in his doggy way, than I love my Jesus.

There is no better time of day for my dog than when I come home. When I am gone, he sits on the sofa and waits for me to come back. It's like a job or a calling.

Then when he hears the car, he waits at the front door. When he sees me, he barks or cries with doggy joy. I unlock the door—he's barking, tail wagging.

He does enjoy other things—squirrels to chase, food, water, certain food items he digs out of the trash—but nothing compares to when I come home. The door opens and we are reunited. It is as if all of life is wrapped up in those singular moments of joy. He greets me as only he can—with a yearning sort of cry, a dance around me or the room.

What are we going to do? he asks. Will you play with me? Feed me? Will we walk together?

I am his master, the source of his food; the one who rubs his tummy, gives him treats, scratches under his chin where his paws cannot reach.

There is no better time to be with him, but others come close. When we wake up in the morning and he sniffs me. When I read in the living room and he sits on the sofa on his pillow. Being where I sit seems to validate him just by my presence. If I reach over and stroke his back, he wags his tail. He delights in my care and any sort of attention that I give. When we have dinner, he sits under the table, hoping like his Gospel counterpart to snag a treat-scrap that falls to the floor.

He delights in any hint of a smell of me that he can find when I'm gone—discarded socks, the chair where I sit, other traces.

It seems to me that he lives to be with me and please me. He takes great joy, maybe the greatest joy, in just being in the house with me.

As for me, I can hear Jesus asking, "Are you still sleeping and taking your rest?"

Crossroad

How can you relate to God more like a devoted dog relates to his owner, and less like the disciples who were convinced of their own faithful strength just before they fell asleep in the garden?

For further reading: Psalm 27:4; Psalm 42.

36

Colors of Eternity

The Pantone 2024 color of the year was Peach Fuzz. Benjamin Moore's paint color of the year was Blue Nova and Behr went with Cracked Pepper.

When I admired a friend's purple sweater, I found out that her church has its own colors of the year, that is the liturgical year—white, purple, violet, red and green. White, the color of Jesus' burial garments, is for Easter and Christmas; purple/violet is for Advent and Lent; red is used in Holy Week and the Day of Pentecost; and green is used during Epiphany and the "Ordinary Time" after Pentecost.

Long before any liturgical year, God's people had their hands full with skeins of blue, purple and scarlet yarn, with fine twined linen and goats' hair. These were to make God a sanctuary, where he could dwell in their midst (see Ex. 25:3-8).

This tabernacle had pillars of acacia wood overlaid with gold, bases of silver and a tent covering of ram skins dyed red. High priestly garments were a coat of checkered work of sardius, topaz, carbuncle, emerald, sapphire, diamonds, jacinth, agate, amethyst, beryl, onyx and jasper (28:17-20). Imagine precious stones catching the candlelight and the holy place exploding in color.

And it was all temporary, but pointing to that lasting city whose designer and builder is God. And what a city he designed—a city full of his glory, "its radiance like a most rare jewel, like a jasper, clear as crystal" (Rev. 21:11).

The city's wall was "built of jasper, while the city was pure gold, like clear glass" (v. 18). Aged Apostle John continues to describe the foundations of the wall adorned with jasper, sapphire, agate, emerald, onyx, carnelian, chrysolite, beryl, topaz, chrysoprase, jacinth and amethyst. The twelve gates were made of a single pearl, and the street of the city was pure gold (vv. 20-21). It's a repeat of the copy, but more. Instead of reflecting candlelight, these precious stones reflect Light from Light, true God from true God.

There's another color at play. It's God's color of eternity—blood red. Red was the shed lamb's blood on the doorposts that held off the angel of death. Moses painted the book of the law, the tent, the vessels used in worship, even the people in swatches of red blood mixed with water, scarlet wool and hyssop (Heb. 9:19-21). Then we see Jesus pouring out his own blood, which drips down the cross. Blood red, atoning blood that removed sin's stains once for all for sinners, for all eternity. English hymnwriter William Cowper wrote:

> "There is a fountain filled with blood
> Drawn from Immanuel's veins;
> And sinners, plunged beneath that flood,
> Lose all their guilty stains."[17]

Just call my color Washed-in-Blood Red.

Crossroad

What is your color for eternity? Have you been washed in Jesus' atoning blood that takes away the guilty stain of sin? Receive Jesus' forgiveness, once for all eternity.

For further reading: Isaiah 1:18.

37

Dots, Lines, Circles ... Eternal Life

Think about written language. Little dots and lines and circles arranged in a certain way make up letters. Letters arranged in different orders become words that represent actual things and thoughts. These words arranged together become sentences to paragraphs to books. That amazes me.

Something or someone got ahold of William Tyndale, and he determined to put the Bible into English and into the hands of the English-speaking people. When William Tyndale translated the New Testament into English, he had to invent new words to express truths for which English, at the time, did not have the exact word he wanted. His translation of the New Testament was completed in 1525.

Eleven years later, Tyndale was condemned as a heretic, strangled and burned at the stake. Yet his work became the basis for future English-language Bibles.

I think of my friend Yousaf Sadiq as a modern-day Tyndale. As a boy in a Muslim-majority country, he woke up each morning to the Muslim call to prayer and to his father singing Christian psalms in their language. Where did his father learn such songs?

Yousaf discovered the prayer songs his father sang were Punjabi-language psalms that were passed down orally from generation to generation. Yousaf began to write them down, along with their history.

These psalms are a core part of every branch of Christian churches in Punjabi-language worship. Yet cultural shifts mean the preferred language for many is Urdu or English. "Punjabi is my mother-tongue," Yousaf told me. "As I studied how these psalms came to be, I began to see who I was as both a Christian and a person."

He wrote a book, *The Contextualized Psalms: A precious heritage of the global Punjabi Christian community.* Yousaf's updated history of the Punjabi psalms and his translation of these psalms were published in Punjabi in 2023. Even as the language itself fades, the psalms can live and move from generation to generation.

Both Tyndale and Sadiq worked in the context of persecution to bring truths to their people in the form of words. Language mattered to both. Tyndale created new words to bring the Bible to life; Yousaf's work brings a persecuted people together in worship like no other words or writing in his homeland.

Whether it's Greek, Hebrew, Punjabi, English or another language, words point us toward God or away from him. Words can be used by God to bring people to Christ or can harm. We are messengers of eternal life.

All things new

Let's choose our words, whether spoken or written, with great care, expressing truth and love. Let's speak and write to those around us reflecting the Word of God. "Heaven and earth will pass away, but my words will not pass away" (Mark 13:31). "The grass withers, the flower fades, but the word of our God will stand forever" (Is. 40:8).

For further reading: John 1:1–4.

38

Missing Lunch

Long ago, airfares dropped between Chicago and London so that it cost less to fly to London than to Los Angeles. So, we found ourselves in London on holiday.

When we travel, we like to be both spontaneous and in control. We made a list of places we wanted to see and things we wanted to do. Sunday afternoon was assigned a specific place, but first was Sunday morning. That meant church.

We went to All Souls Church. Back then, John Stott was the rector. We got there on time and had a seat. We could see that there was some community life in this church, that it was a lot more than just the church where John Stott preached. We felt more or less at home. This happens in other parts of the world, too, so it's not just an English-speaking thing. Even if we don't understand the language where we're worshiping, we're at home.

At the end of the service, we started talking to a man. He was a regular attender. We answered his questions, and he seemed especially keen on our missionary background. We clicked with him. We didn't want to stop talking and neither did he.

Then, he invited us to his home for lunch. What were we to do with this unexpected invitation? We were on holiday, and Sunday morning may have meant church, but Sunday afternoon, well, that meant a museum or a gallery or a park. We explained that we had our plans. He understood and wished us well. We parted ways.

Looking back, I don't recall what places we visited that Sunday after church. What I do remember is that kind man's invitation and I wonder what that Sunday lunch may have held for us. We will never know. I like to think that I am different nowadays, choosing the family of God over the art, artifacts and trinkets of human achievement.

Jesus accepted dinner invitations from tax collectors, sinners or Pharisees, and he always brought the unexpected to the table. In Luke 14, Jesus was dining with a ruler of the Pharisees. It almost sounds as if the Pharisees were anticipating the unexpected from Jesus as they carefully watched him (v. 1), and Jesus didn't disappoint them. After calling out the Pharisees for their hypocrisy and pride of place, he turned to his host with a guest list for his next dinner: "when you give a feast, invite the poor, the crippled, the lame, the blind, and you will be blessed, because they cannot repay you. For you will be repaid at the resurrection of the just" (vv. 13-14).

One day we will sit down with that man from All Souls. Jesus opens the door and invites us in. He serves a feast—lamb seasoned with spices and placed on a table with freshly washed and neatly folded linens.

All things new

Next time, accept or extend that unexpected invitation to lunch or supper.

For further reading: Mark 3:31-35.

39

Social-Distancing Death

Living through the Covid pandemic forced people to confront death. When I think of death, I end up thinking about some of my best friends in life who have died.

I think of Jim. The best man in my wedding—and I was the best man in his—he was a youth pastor, magician, puppeteer, trombonist, master of the pun and corny jokes, and Christian ministry professor. Jim just got me in a way that is hard to describe. People appreciate me, they like me, but with Jim, it clicked. He just got me.

One day he was walking with his wife, and his leg went numb. He thought he was having a stroke. But it turned out to be inoperable brain cancer.

I did my best to walk with him through that, even though I was here in Illinois and he was out in California. I called him most nights, and we checked with each other on how things were going. Then, when he couldn't talk anymore, his wife would tell me what was going on. Toward the end, he said he saw Jesus in the room with him, praying. And then he went to heaven. For me, there's no replacing Jim.

There's also Peter. He was the missionary force that God used to put my heart in Russia and Ukraine, to serve the church there. Mostly, though,

Peter was a man who wanted to do everything he could to help other people know and follow Jesus. I was part of a handful of people who worked here in Wheaton while he lived in Moscow.

Then, out of nowhere, he was heading to Mayo Clinic. His lymphoma was aggressive and fast. He fought hard. We prayed hard. Peter's energy, humility and ministry partnership with his wife have shaped me and Lorraine in ways that I can't even begin to express. For me, there's no replacing Peter.

Death is the enemy. Even Jesus prayed for the cup to pass if there was any other way. Of course, when we die, we won't be taking the sins of the world on ourselves as he did, so his cup is a lot different than the ones we will all drink.

I miss these friends more than I can say. My life felt better with them physically here. The grief of losing them doesn't end. But Jesus called them home. I trust him.

We aren't people of death. We Christians are about life. The hymn isn't "Jesus Died and So Shall I." It's "Jesus Lives and So Shall I." That means that I will see Jim and Peter again. That day will be richer and fuller than we can imagine. We'll see Jesus and one another at the same time and cry out together, "Come. Drink. Live."

Pray out loud

> "Worthy are you, our Lord and God,
> to receive glory and honor and power,
> for you created all things,
> and by your will they existed and were created."

(Revelation 4:11)

For further reading: 1 Corinthians 15:20-22.

40

Second Day

A new day was coming. Feeding thousands with next to nothing. Saying someone was taking a nap when she was dead. And then—at Jesus' word—she starts walking, just as a man walks out of his own tomb.

When Jesus talked about being lifted up, they thought it would be on some sort of royal dais. Exalted. It never occurred to them that he meant being nailed and lifted up on a cross.

He was arrested and crucified; they scattered, denied, hid behind closed doors, prayed, wondered, wept. That Easter Sunday shocked them all. When they woke that morning, they were in despair. Big events in life change people.

Angels appeared. The gardener turned out to be so much more. Jesus was suddenly in their midst. Thomas, though doubting, got to touch his wounds. Thomas changed—not by knowledge, but by truth experienced through face-to-face events. Jesus cooked them breakfast on the beach. He walked on the road with them and explained. They watched Jesus go up into heaven, staring until someone asked what they were doing.

Sunday wasn't Sunday anymore. It was Resurrection Day. Their week changed. Every day when they woke up, they would remember. He was dead and then he was alive. Then they saw him go up into the sky. It was the day to gather, worship, remember, celebrate. To mark the Last Supper again, remembering what Jesus said. It didn't make sense then, but now it did.

So every week they began together. The disciples took to the road and the seas, going everywhere, telling everyone that Jesus and Spirit and Father all live and rule. Forgiveness and life are real, out there and in here, and lasting forever. The gospel news is that Jesus was and is alive.

These men would be regarded as criminals because of him, arrested, beaten, exiled, killed. There's another way to live, and another way to die and live again.

> "On Second Day morn, they knew.
> They took up their crosses,
> Created the creeds.
> The people of God took care of all needs.
> It was not a war. It was a new world,
> Though Rome all around them swirled.
> Battles raged; the war was already won
> On the cross, at the tomb and in the sky that's all.
> This truth and beauty is our Second Day call.
> Unspotted Lamb,
> Eternal Shepherd,
> One.
> Only alive and ever
> Triumphant forever.
> Father,
> Spirit,
> Son."[18]

Pray out loud

Pray for someone who needs to hear about the "second day."

For further reading: Acts 2:32-36.

Notes

1 Leland Ryken, *The Heart in Pilgrimage: A Treasury of Classic Devotions on the Christian Life* (Crossway, 2022), p. 73.

2 C.S. Lewis, *Mere Christianity* (HarperOne, copyright renewed 1980), p. 122.

3 Voice of the Martyrs, *Foxe Voices of the Martyrs: AD33–Today* (VOM Books, 2022), p. 140.

4 Jancee Dunn, “Make Something with Your Hands (Even if It’s Hideous)” in *The New York Times*, 30 June 2024.

5 Andrew Das, Sarah Lyall and Kris Rhim, “Buddy Holly, petit basset griffon Vendéen, wins best in show at Westminster Kennel Club Dog Show” in *The New York Times*, 9 May 2023.

6 Smithsonian Channel, *Aerial America*, “Yellowstone” (series 8, episode 2).

7 John Rippon, “How Firm a Foundation” (1787).

8 Samuel Crossman, “My Song Is Love Unknown” (1664).

9 Lilly Blomquist, “ Wedding Guests Required to Purchase $333 Tickets to Attend Couple’s New York City Nuptials” in *Brides*, 31 July 2024.

10 Dana Smith, “Why Gardening Is So Good for You” in *The New York Times*, 23 May 2024.

11 John Milton, *Paradise Lost: Book 1* (1674).

12 Merriam-Webster, “Where Does the Expression ‘Throw Someone Under the Bus’ Come From?” <https://www.merriam-webster.com/wordplay/why-do-we-throw-someone-under-the-bus>

13 Eleanor Cummins and Andrew Zaleski, “If Loneliness Is an Epidemic, How Do We Treat It?” in *The New York Times*, 14 July 2023.

14 Charles Wesley, “Christ the Lord is Risen Today” (1739).

15 Tim Herrera, “Let Go of Your Grudges. They’re Doing You No Good” in *The New York Times*, 19 May 2019.

16 Dr Frederic Luskin, Stanford Forgiveness Project (1999), <https://livehappy.com/practice/9-steps-to-forgiveness/>

17 William Cowper, “There Is a Fountain Filled with Blood” (1772).

18 These words are written by Wil Triggs.

Acknowledgments

Our families are breathing in the pages of this book.

Our parents and especially our siblings and their spouses were source material for many of these devotionals. They laughed at us and with us as we learned to laugh at ourselves and the world.

Our missions family also give life to these pages. Friends and colleagues at Russian Ministries/Mission Eurasia, Slavic Gospel Association, World Evangelical Alliance and Media Associates International opened our eyes to the world in which Jesus is moving every moment of every day.

Our church family made this book possible. College Church (Wheaton, IL) has supported us as short-term and career missionaries, allowed us to teach children, hone our communication skills and serve them in many other capacities. Born out of the Saturday devotionals we write for the church each week, this book comes from our shared worship and service over many years. We want to thank the people of our church who read and share them week by week and have been asking, "When are you going to put these in a book?"

Thank you Trish Main, Jonathan Pountney and Julie Hatherall, for making us better writers as we finalized the manuscript.